W9-BWA-706

SOCIAL
MEDIA
SENSATIONS

Vine

Jill C. Wheeler

Checkerboard
Library

An Imprint of Abdo Publishing
abdopublishing.com

abdopublishing.com

Published by Abdo Publishing, a division of ABDO, PO Box 398166, Minneapolis, Minnesota 55439. Copyright © 2017 by Abdo Consulting Group, Inc. International copyrights reserved in all countries. No part of this book may be reproduced in any form without written permission from the publisher. Checkerboard Library™ is a trademark and logo of Abdo Publishing.

Printed in the United States of America, North Mankato, Minnesota
062016
092016

THIS BOOK CONTAINS
RECYCLED MATERIALS

Design: Emily Love, Mighty Media, Inc.
Production: Mighty Media, Inc.
Editor: Liz Salzmann
Cover Photos: Shutterstock
Interior Photos: AP Images, pp. 11, 14, 21; Getty Images, pp. 5, 9, 13, 17, 19; iStockphoto, pp. 6, 7, 15, 25, 29; Shutterstock, pp. 4, 23, 27

Publishers Cataloging-in-Publication Data
Names: Wheeler, Jill C., author.
Title: Vine / by Jill C. Wheeler.
Description: Minneapolis, MN : Abdo Publishing, [2017] | Series: Social media
    sensations | Includes index.
Identifiers: LCCN 2016934278 | ISBN 9781680781946 (lib. bdg.) |
    ISBN 9781680775792 (ebook)
Subjects: LCSH: Online social networks--Juvenile literature. | Internet
    industry--United States--Juvenile literature.
 Classification: DDC 658.872--dc23
LC record available at /http://lccn.loc.gov/2016934278

Contents

Vine

URL: http://vine.co

PURPOSE: Vine is a video-sharing website and **mobile** app. Users can watch, **upload**, share, and comment on short, looping video clips.

CURRENT CEO: Jack Dorsey

NUMBERS OF USERS: more than 200 million

JUNE 2012
Vine is founded

OCTOBER 2012
Twitter acquires Vine

AUGUST 2013
Vine reaches
40 million users

JANUARY 2015
VineKids is launched

Meet the Founders

DOM HOFMANN worked for the travel website company Jetsetter before co-founding Vine. That is where he met Yusupov and Kroll. Hofmann served as lead general manager of Vine until 2014.

RUS YUSUPOV has a degree in graphic arts from the School of Visual Arts in New York City. After graduating, he worked for several Internet companies, including Jetsetter. Yusupov was the creative director of Vine until 2015.

COLIN KROLL attended Oakland University in Rochester, Michigan. He met Hofmann and Yusupov while working for Jetsetter. Kroll was general manager of Vine until 2014.

CHAPTER 1

What Is Vine?

You and a friend create a funny **skit**. Your mom films and edits it on her cell phone. Soon, it is ready to post on Vine. The catch? The entire video can only be six seconds long! Instantly, your friends watch and comment on the video. That's Vine in action!

Vine is a **mobile** video-sharing service. Vine users, or Viners, create and post short videos called vines. Vines can also be **uploaded** to other sites, including Twitter, Facebook, and Tumblr.

Upon opening the Vine app, Viners see videos posted by users they follow.

Viners create videos of all kinds, but making funny vines is very popular.

Vine is unlike any other video-sharing service. Each vine is limited to just six seconds. These short clips play on constant loops. They offer brief peeks into the worlds of their creators.

CHAPTER 2

Vine Is Born

Vine is the creation of three tech pioneers. They are Dom Hofmann, Rus Yusupov, and Colin Kroll. Before starting Vine, all three worked for travel website company Jetsetter in New York City. While there, the trio discussed ideas for creating a new tech business.

In June 2012, Hofmann, Yusupov, and Kroll settled on an idea. They built a video tool. It allowed users to film and combine any number of short videos.

After showing the tool to friends, the creators noticed something. Many users were texting their videos to each other. So, the men realized what their app needed. Its content had to be quick and easy to share.

Did You Know?

Vine's name is from the word *vignette* (vin-YET). A vignette is a short scene.

Vine co-founders Rus Yusupov (left) *and Colin Kroll* (right)
at the 2014 Variety *Breakthrough of the Year Awards*

The longer a video is, the longer it can take to **upload**. So, Hofmann, Yusupov, and Kroll began testing video lengths. The ideal video would be short to allow speedy uploads. But it would still be long enough to make sense. The founders also felt limitations would make people more creative. Short videos would force users to think up new ways of filming and editing.

CHAPTER 3

Looping Videos

Yusupov, Hofmann, and Kroll experimented with different video lengths. Ten seconds and nine seconds felt too long. They also tried five seconds. But it didn't feel long enough to share an idea.

The founders finally settled on six seconds. It was long enough to tell a short, entertaining story. And six seconds kept the videos short enough to be quickly **downloaded** and viewed.

However, there was one problem. The founders felt disappointed when the short, exciting clips ended. So, they added another distinctive feature to their app. Each Vine video

Did You Know?

Six seconds is the official length of Vine videos. But they can actually be 6.5 seconds long. The founders wanted to give users an extra half second if needed.

Marutaro is a Japanese hedgehog who has starred in many vines. He has more than 50,000 followers on Vine!

repeats in a constant loop. These short, looping videos set Vine apart from other video-sharing services. Now, the founders just needed their app to take off.

CHAPTER 4

Twitter Takes Over

Vine was created in June 2012. At first, the app was only offered to a small number of users. It was not **available** publicly. However, the app still caught the attention of another major social media site.

Early in development, Vine's founders had met with social media site Twitter. Vine's founders wanted to share their videos on Twitter. This discussion soon led to talks of acquisition. Twitter was looking to add video sharing to its service. The company recognized Vine as something special, and wanted to buy it.

In fall 2012, Twitter purchased Vine for $30 million. Kroll, Hofmann, and Yusupov continued to run the company. That October, Vine was released publicly as its own site. It was also made Twitter's official video-posting service. Now, anyone age 17 and older could create a Vine account. Signing up was even easier for Twitter users.

Twitter's headquarters in San Francisco, California. In 2015, Twitter opened offices in New York, sharing a building with Vine.

Vine's public launch was a success. It was instantly introduced to the millions of Twitter users. By June 2013, Vine had 13 million users, or Viners. By August, there were more than 40 million Viners.

Like Vine, Twitter also limits the length of posts. Twitter messages can have up to 140 characters. These brief posts perfectly **complemented** Vine's short videos.

CHAPTER 5

Using Vine

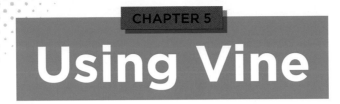

Viners can easily create and post short, entertaining videos. First, users sign up with an e-mail address or Twitter account. Next, they create a profile and username. They can also write a little about themselves.

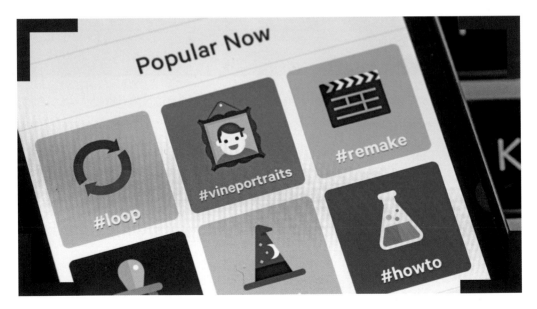

Vine has a special Popular Now section that groups vines with trending hashtags.

A Viner can find friends by searching for their usernames. Then, he or she can follow these users. Following allows a Viner to see any videos his or her friends post.

Users can add hashtags to their vines. A hashtag is the hash symbol (#) followed by a word or phrase. Hashtags can be used to search for similar videos. So, a vine of a cute dog could have the hashtag #cutedogs. Tapping the hashtag lets the user see more vines with cute dogs.

Film and Stitch

To film a vine, users must use a **mobile** device. The users press and hold the camera icon on their screen within the app. The app will continue to film for up to 6.5 seconds. If the user removes his or her finger, filming pauses. Users can rearrange the scene in between clips. They can then stitch these clips together. Users can also edit and reorder clips.

CHAPTER 6

Vine Culture

As Vine gained more and more users, it developed a growing Internet **culture**. The app's time limit and loop feature worked especially well for comedy. Vine soon became known for its community of comedic users posting funny videos.

Making people laugh in six seconds can be challenging. Viners must create their own brand of comedy to be successful. Funny vines range from silly to magical to strange.

Some vines go **viral**. They are viewed again and again. These videos are shared by users billions of times.

Did You Know?

Viners can combine their best vines into longer videos. These can be posted on the video-sharing site YouTube. YouTube accepts longer videos than Vine.

Andrew Bachelor (left) *has appeared in five episodes of the TV show* The Mindy Project *since becoming famous on Vine.*

Some Viners whose videos **consistently** go **viral** have become famous. One such star is Andrew Bachelor, whose username is KingBach. He has more than 14 million followers. His videos have earned more than 5 billion loop views. Bachelor was able to turn this fame into an acting career. He has guest starred on several television shows.

CHAPTER 7

New Talent

Vine has also helped new musicians. These musicians post clips of themselves performing. Musical vines are viewed and shared, increasing the artist's exposure. Like Vine comedians, some of these artists have turned their fame on Vine into a career.

In 2013, Viner Shawn Mendes posted a video of himself singing and playing guitar. The clip received 10,000 views overnight! By the next year, Mendes had more than 3 million followers. He also had a contract to produce a record.

The entertainment industry now uses Vine to find new talent. If a vine becomes popular quickly, it is a good sign that its creator appeals to fans. Many entertainers discovered on Vine have built successful careers.

The first vine Shawn Mendes posted was a six-second cover of Justin Bieber's song "As Long as You Love Me."

CHAPTER 9

News and Campaigns

Vine's millions of users have become a powerful force. Their viewing and sharing has turned popular Viners into stars. It has created successful ad campaigns. Users can also share breaking news and support social issues.

On April 15, 2013, tragedy struck at the Boston Marathon in Massachusetts. Bombs exploded at the finish line of race. Vine helped the news of the bombing spread around the world.

Doug Lorman was there and filmed the explosion on Vine. He then shared it on Twitter. The video was viewed more than 40,000 times. This proved that Vine could be used for more than entertainment. It could be a genuine news source.

Vine is also being used for social media campaigns. In 2015, First Lady Michelle Obama launched her Reach Higher **initiative**. It aims to inspire students to complete

People laying memorials for victims of the Boston Marathon bombing. Viners posted 19,667 videos on the day of the bombing.

some form of higher education after high school. Part of this **initiative** is the Better Make Room campaign.

This campaign uses social media to celebrate high-school students and their efforts to succeed. Vine will ask popular Viners to create videos for the campaign. The goal of the vines will be to encourage students and **showcase** successful young people.

CHAPTER 10

Managing Content

Whether making people laugh or supporting social campaigns, Vine inspires positivity. However, its content is not always positive. And it is not always **appropriate** for all viewers.

Vine users must be 17 to have an account. But anyone can visit Vine's website and watch Vine videos. And Vine has no rules about what users can **upload**. Soon after the app launched, some users began posting **inappropriate** videos.

Vine still does not review videos before they are posted. But it did make changes in 2013. The site now blocks videos with hashtags that indicate mature content.

In 2015, Vine took another step toward cleaner content. That January, VineKids was launched as a separate app. Vine previews the app's videos before they are posted. It makes sure they are family-friendly. In addition, VineKids

VineKids allows families to watch vines together without worrying inappropriate content will appear.

videos have an interactive twist. Young users can **swipe** left or right for more videos. They can also tap the videos on their screens to hear fun sound effects.

CHAPTER 11

Vine's Future

Today's Vine community is large and **diverse**. It includes comedians, musicians, artists, and filmmakers. Vine is used to share creativity and discover new talent. Meanwhile, Vine's owners have continued to improve the app based on user interests.

In 2013, Vine added channel pages. These make it easier to search for vines by content. Users can visit different comedy, music, and dance channels. There they can see the top videos of those **categories**.

Another way Vine has responded to its users likes and needs is with music. Many Viners want to add background music to their vines. This previously had to been done using a separate app. In 2015, Vine added Snap to Beat, a new music feature. With this tool, a Viner can choose a song from his or her device's music library. Snap to Beat then pairs six seconds of the song to the video.

Every day, people find new, creative ways to use Vine to entertain and inform their followers.

With new app tools and user ideas, the Vine community is sure to continue advancing. It will create more amazing projects, comedic sketches, and famous stars. And the world will be watching, six seconds at a time!

A GUIDE TO
Vine

A Vine user must be at least 17 to have an account.

Vine users create a profile. This includes their name and an e-mail address or Twitter account.

To follow friends on Vine, users can search for their usernames. They can also search for popular Viners to follow. These can be found by searching for trending hashtags or in the Popular Now video tab.

To record a video in Vine, users press the camera icon. It is found in the top-right corner of the app. Users hold their finger on the screen and begin recording. The app will continue recording until the user removes his or her finger.

After recording a video, users can watch it. They just tap the arrow in the top-right corner of their screen. They can then rearrange their clips by tapping the edit button. This allows them to drag the clips in a new order.

It is important Viners use the app safely. They should never post or revine **inappropriate** content. And they should never share information people could use to find them in real life. This includes an address or phone number.

Glossary

appropriate – suitable, fitting, or proper.

available – able to be had or used.

category – a group of people or things that are similar in some way.

complement – to fit well with something else or make it better.

consistent – continuing to happen or develop in the same way.

culture – the customs, arts, and tools of a nation or a people at a certain time.

diverse – made up of people who are different from one another.

download – to transfer data from a computer network to a single computer or device.

inappropriate – not suitable, fitting, or proper.

initiative – a plan or program that is intended to solve a problem.

merchandise – goods that are bought and sold.

mobile – capable of moving or being moved.

potential – a quality that something has that can be developed or used.

showcase – to exhibit something to try to get others to like it.

skit – a short, funny play or performance.

swipe – to drag one or more fingers across the screen of a smartphone or tablet.

upload – to transfer data from a computer to a larger network.

viral – quickly or widely spread, usually by electronic communication.

Websites

To learn more about Social Media Sensations, visit **booklinks.abdopublishing.com**. These links are routinely monitored and updated to provide the most current information available.

Index